lonely planet
Kids

Adventures in Noisy Places

Packed full of Activities and over 250 Stickers

This noisy little howler monkey is hiding in every main sticker scene. Can you find him?

NoisyWORLD

Wow! This is a map of the world. It shows all the noisy places in your book.

LONDON, UK

AUSTRIA

MONA

SUPER BOWL, USA

THE AMAZON

The Amazon

IGUAÇU NATIONAL PARK, BRAZIL

Count how many ships and animals there are bobbing in the water. Can you see a shark, a dolphin, and a speedboat?

There's a flag for each noisy place you'll be exploring. Find the matching stickers at the end of your book and stick them in the right places.

RUSSIA

HONG KONG

MAURITIUS

SYDNEY, AUSTRALIA

3

READY TO GO!

Make an adventure pass to explore noisy places!
Write your name and age, draw your picture, and then add your country stamp stickers.

MY NOISY ADVENTURE PASS

Draw your face here.

Name *Sophia Sofia*

Age *8*

Stick your country stamps here.

NOISY PLACES POSTCARD

Draw something you find noisy. Then write the name of someone to send your postcard to.

ZOO

Roo B

Don't forget to draw a stamp!

Hi

USA

Americans can travel on the highway, the subway, and through the air, taking them overground and underground.

America's national bird, the bald eagle, can soar high in the sky to get a bird's-eye view of everyone below.

DONT WALK
WALK

Street signs tell you when you can cross the street and when it is the cars' turn to go.

Add some passengers to the yellow taxi. Quick, the meter is ticking away!

5

The very first Super Bowl was played in 1967. Over 100 million people now watch the Super Bowl on television each year.

SCORE

HOME : GUEST
T.O.L. T.O.L.
DOWN TO GO BALL ON QTR

TOUCHDOWN!

The fans clap, cheer, and yell. Sometimes the stadium gets too noisy for the players to hear each other!

Add stickers to make the game fun.

Cheerleaders wear bright uniforms when they cheer and dance to support their team. Can you make sure they have pom-poms to shake?

PER BOWL

THE SUPER BOWL is the championship game of the National Football League. It is played in a different city every year and is the most watched game in the country.

Go team!

HOTDOGS

Football players are big, tall, and strong, but they still wear helmets and special padded clothing for protection.

LET'S PLAY BALL!

Three of the most popular sports in America are baseball, basketball, and football. Can you paint the gloves, bats, and balls?

In football, players try to score points by running or passing the ball down the field. They can also score points by kicking the ball through a goalpost.

Baseball players hit the ball with the bat and run as hard as they can around the bases. The other team tries to catch the ball with their gloves.

Incredibly tall basketball players dart around the court, bouncing and passing the ball and throwing it through a high hoop. Swish!

8

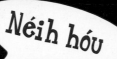

Néih hóu

CHINA

Welcome to China! Over a billion people live here – and so do some cuddly giant pandas. It's also home to the greatest Great Wall ever.

Giant pandas are furry black and white bears from the forested mountains of central China. They sit upright to eat bamboo and spend the rest of their day sleeping.

The huge seated Buddha on Lantau Island, called Tian Tan, is made of bronze. It has a bell inside that rings 108 times a day.

Can you add some delicious food to this bowl of noodles?

Get on board the **STAR FERRY**, which transports noisy passengers across Victoria Harbour in Hong Kong. The journey offers amazing views of the city.

STAR FERRY

Passengers make lots of noise, chatting and joking. Some are tourists, and others are locals. Can you put more people on board?

Boom! Boom! The captain sounds his horn as a warning to other boats.

碼頭 →

CHINESE LANTERNS

Chinese lanterns are made from paper. They light up the sky during the spring Lantern Festival.

At festival time in China, children carry paper lanterns made in the shape of animals and decorated with beautiful images.

Chinese lanterns are mostly bright red and are believed to bring good luck to everybody as they float in the sky. Can you make the lanterns light up?

Hello

UNITED KINGDOM

London is the capital of the United Kingdom. It is one of the world's most exciting cities, where people bustle around famous landmarks old and new.

The Shard is western Europe's tallest building. It has 72 floors and is covered in 11,000 glass panels. It is shaped like a shard of glass, or a tall thin pyramid, and is filled with offices, restaurants, apartments, and a hotel.

The London Eye is a large observation wheel with 32 glass cabins. Each cabin carries 26 passengers, all hoping for a fantastic view of the city as they ride above the River Thames.

It's teatime. Add some milk, dunk a yummy treat, and give it a stir!

Use your stickers to make the scene even noisier.
Members of the House of Lords sit on red benches. They are usually calm and quiet, but they can get very noisy!
Guess who was in the back of my cab last week!
The Queen visits Parliament each year to give a speech. Everybody stops making a noise and listens very carefully. Shhhh!

THE HOUSES OF PARLIAMENT,

where British laws are made, can be found inside the Palace of Westminster. Politicians come here for very noisy discussions with each other, so bring your earplugs!

THE CROWN JEWELS

The Crown Jewels are kept at the Tower of London, but the Queen wears the Imperial State Crown once a year, when she opens Parliament.

Rubies are red, sapphires are blue, emeralds are green – and diamonds sparkle most of all! Can you decorate each jewel?

This crown was worn by Queen Victoria and is completely covered in diamonds. Can you make it shine?

Privyet

RUSSiA

Russia is famous for ballet dancing, a group of buildings called the Kremlin (where the Russian President lives), and the Trans-Siberian Railway.

Moscow's world-famous Bolshoi Ballet is full of strong, athletic dancers. The women, called ballerinas, dance on tiptoe, and the men lift them up into the air.

The Trans-Siberian Railway crosses Russia and connects it to Mongolia, China, and North Korea. The journey from Moscow to Russia's Pacific Coast lasts six days and is the longest in the world. Choo! Choo!

Quick! Stick a hat on each passenger's head to help them keep warm.

Add some stickers to the explosive scene!

Satellites are launched into orbit above Earth. The largest is the International Space Station. Other satellites can send television and phone signals around the world.

The first animal in space was a type of husky dog named Laika. She was launched on board the spacecraft Sputnik 2. In English, her name means 'barker'. Woof!

18

Russian astronauts are called cosmonauts. They blast off for outer space in rockets launched from **THE BAIKONUR COSMODROME**, which is in Kazakhstan. The noise is deafening!

Russia's first space station, called Mir, was home to teams from around the world. Today, very noisy rockets fly supplies to the International Space Station. It is the size of a football field!

OUR SOLAR SYSTEM

The Solar System is a collection of eight planets, including Earth. The Sun is in the middle.

SATURN

NEPTUNE

VENUS

THE SUN

URANUS

MERCURY

All of the planets move around the Sun. It is a star that creates heat, light, and energy. Can you make it shine?

EARTH

The other planets are so far away from Earth that it would take many years to reach them. Can you make them all look different?

MARS

JUPITER

Oi

BRAZIL

Brazil is home to a gigantic mountaintop statue called Christ the Redeemer, a huge sports stadium called Maracanã, and an enormous party called the Rio Carnival. It's time to samba!

About one-third of all the world's coffee comes from Brazil. But did you know that the original plants were from Ethiopia in Africa?

The world's biggest carnival is held in Rio de Janeiro's Sambadrome and throughout the city. It is a five-day festival of music, singing, and dancing.

Sugarloaf Mountain is next to Guanabara Bay in Rio. You can reach the top in a glass cable car and get a sky-high view of the city below.

Feed the Brazilian horned frog with some tasty flies, but keep your boots on – he might try to taste your toes!

The bright pink Belmond Hotel das Cataratas faces Iguaçu Falls. Guests can visit the falls even after everybody else has gone home.

Add a splash to the scene with your stickers!

The water makes a thundering sound as it drops 82 m (269 ft.) and hits the river below. Boom!

There is a spectacular series of cascading waterfalls in **iGUAÇU NATiONAL PARK,** between Brazil and Argentina. The powerful spray can be heard from a great distance. Whoosh!

Approaching the falls on a jet boat is thrilling. You can hear the roar of the water as you get near – and then feel it when you get splashed!

The rainforest in Iguaçu is home to tapirs and giant anteaters with long snouts. Very nosy creatures!

SQUAWKI G PARROTS

There are over 300 types of parrots, including macaws, cockatoos, and lorikeets. They have brightly decorated feathers.

They make fantastic pets and can be excellent mimics, often singing with a loud, clear voice. Squawk! Squawk!

Can you paint all the parrots? Who's a pretty boy, then!

In Austria you'll find snowy mountains called Alps, scrumptious cakes called strudel, and the very noisy Vegetable Orchestra!

Guten tag

AUSTRIA

Use your stickers to give the children hats and skis.

Vienna's Ferris wheel, called the Riesenrad, is taller than the wingspan of a jumbo jet. You can ride the big wheel and watch the world go round.

Vienna's Schönbrunn Palace is a mansion surrounded by beautiful gardens and a maze. Visitors listen to Mozart and Strauss concerts in the palace – if they can get out of the maze in time!

They perform around the world, from Moscow to Singapore.

Celery, artichokes, pumpkins, and even onion skins can become musical instruments. Imagine how loud your dinner could be!

Quick, before the music starts, fill the stage with vegetables!

This orchestra plays very tasty music.

Their first instrument was made from a tomato, which is really a fruit. After the concert, the audience is served vegetable soup. Perhaps the musicians should sing for their supper?

Live tonight,
VIENNA'S VEGETABLE ORCHESTRA!
The music is about to begin.
Are you hungry yet?

Their instruments include a leek violin, a cucumber phone, and a carrot recorder. How many noisy vegetable instruments can you see?

WONDERFUL HUNDERTWASSER HOUSE

The artist Friedensreich Hundertwasser turned a very dull Vienna apartment building into the strange but wonderful Hundertwasser House.

The building can be replastered every year, which allows children to write and draw on the walls. What fun to use a building as a sketch pad! Can you draw something on the Hundertwasser House?

The House has bright, shiny, lumpy walls with uneven floors. Every level is a different height and every window a different size, and the building is covered with plants and trees, like a huge, decorated tree house.

28

Hola

Green anacondas, the world's largest snakes, are longer and wider than a human being! They hide in shallow water and squeeze their visitors. Tread carefully or you might get a big hug!

THE AMAZON

The Amazon

The Amazon flows through South America's rainforests and is home to piranha fish and anaconda snakes. Beside the river, people live high up in stilt houses to avoid becoming a fish supper!

Fill your bag with gloves, an alpaca hat, and Peruvian panpipes.

Peruvian stilt houses are made from wood and woven palms found in the rainforest. They have open window frames without any glass. That's natural air conditioning.

Add your stickers and make the rainforest even noisier!

Howlers are the biggest monkeys in the Amazon. They have beards and very long black, brown, or red hair.

HOWLER MONKEYS are the noisiest animals in the Amazon rainforest. You can hear them through thick trees from 5 km (3 mi.) away, which is about an hour's walk.

They eat leaves, fruit, and flowers from high up in the treetops, gripping the branches with their tails. Just hanging out with friends!

They howl to protect their home and food from other troops of monkeys – the loudest burglar alarm ever!

RAINFOREST CREATURES

Trees in the Amazon produce the oxygen that rainforest creatures like frogs, snakes, and spiders need to breathe.

The rainforest is full of boa constrictor snakes and poison dart frogs. The frogs are very bright to frighten their enemies. Can you make the frog on this page a scary-looking orange and blue?

Can you spy some spiders? Tarantulas have hairy bodies and legs and can grow as big as a dinner plate.

AUSTRALIA

G'day, mate

Australia is flying!
Flying doctors flying planes,
flying foxes flying fast,
flying boomerangs flying
back, and flying flies flying
into everybody!

Koalas are furry marsupials that
carry their babies in a pouch.
They eat eucalyptus leaves and
snooze in the trees all day long.
What a great life!

Flying doctors use
small aircraft to
cross Australia,
treating sick people
who cannot reach
the hospital.

Use your stickers
to decorate the
boomerang with
Aboriginal patterns.

Add some stickers to light up the scene!

Hoot, hoot! The boats on the water blast their horns. Maybe they want to join the party?

HAPPY NEW YEAR

34

on New Year's Eve is one of the noisiest noisy places in the world. Singers sing, crowds cheer, boats blast, and rockets roar!

On December 31 at midnight, seven tons of fireworks explode over Sydney Harbour. That's the same weight as seven cars! Happy New Year!

La, La, Laaaa! Opera singers make an amazing high-pitched noise when they reach their top notes. How high can you sing?

FLYING FOXES

Flying foxes are big bats that communicate with their voices and can see in the dark. How batty is that?

In Australia, flying foxes can be black, grey, red, or even spectacled – which means the fur around their eyes looks like a big pair of glasses. Can you make them all look different?

Flying foxes are also known as fruit bats. They use their strong sense of smell and night vision to find food in the dark, including fruit and flowers. Can you guess what you are eating when you have your eyes closed?

Hello and bonjour

MAURITIUS

The dodo used to live here but couldn't fly. It didn't need to, because it had no enemies on the island.

They speak English, French, and Creole on Mauritius. Here you will find orchids, sugar cane, and sandy beaches, but you won't find a dodo – it's a bird that doesn't exist anymore.

The talipot palm blooms only once in its lifetime. It produces a flower 6 m (20 ft.) long. That's about the height of a giraffe!

Is something bugging you? Add some insect stickers to the orchid.

Grand Bay is a great place for sailing, but in a storm the water gets murky and the wind makes the boats hard to control!

Splish, splosh, splash! The heavy rain is very noisy and creates big puddles of water on the ground. Don't stay out long in this weather!

Whoosh! In a tropical storm the wind howls, the trees sway from side to side, and the sugar cane bends over and touches the ground.

Add your stormy stickers to the wild and windy scene.

During the cyclone season, heavy storms produce dark clouds, wind, and rain, which is very noisy! It's blowing a gale – take cover!

Fishermen catch blue marlin and yellow-fin tuna near Mauritius, but they don't sail in a storm. The waves get too high and the boats begin to sway.

BEAUTiFUL SEASHELLS

Many sea creatures, including scallops and sea snails, have a protective outer skin called a shell. The shells can wash up on the seashore after the animals die.

Beachcombers visit the coastline to collect shells when the tide is out. Can you see any shiny seashells on the seashore?

Can you decorate all the shells?

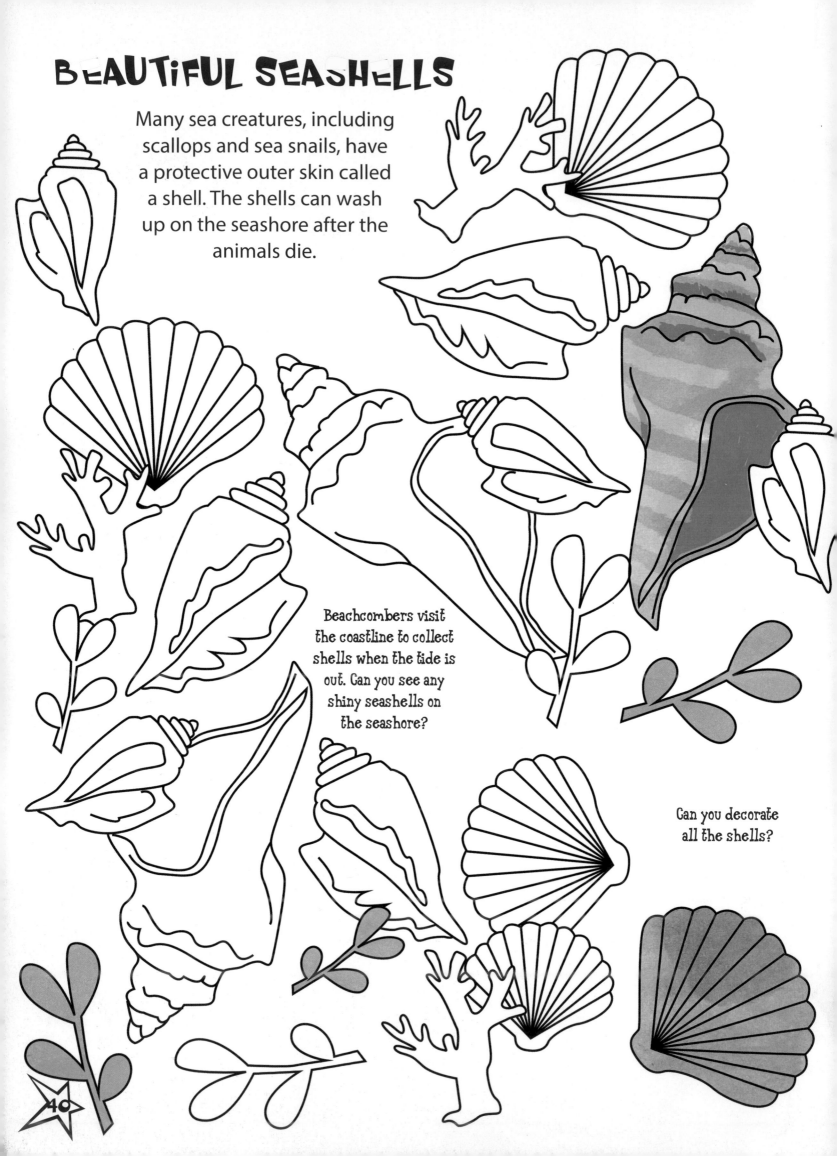

Bonjour

MONACO

Monaco, a tiny country bordering France, is home to the Oceanographic Museum, the Prince's Palace, and a world-famous car race, the Monaco Grand Prix.

A cap decorated with laurel leaves is given to winning drivers when they stand on the victory podium after the race. Hooray!

The Oceanographic Museum, high up above the sea, has around 100 pools inside, allowing you to visit the world's oceans without even getting wet!

Give the people in the boat snorkels and a waterproof camera to take some photos.

41

Add your stickers to make the scene rock!

Vroom, vroom! The cars make lots of noise when they get going.

LES VOITURES

The cars speed around the track for 78 laps, passing the port and the Hotel de Paris. They even roar through a tunnel.

The crowds shout, cheer, and applaud when the drivers pass by. The noise can be deafening! How loudly can you cheer?

The entire country becomes a racing track for the **MONACO GRAND PRIX,** which is the hardest and most important Formula One race in the world. Watch carefully – they drive so fast you might miss them!

During the Grand Prix, lucky people with big yachts watch the race and yell excitedly from their decks.

UNDERWATER WONDERWORLD

Explore this underwater world filled with animals from Monaco's amazing Oceanographic Museum.

Find the jellyfish and paint them pink. Find the shells and paint them red. How many starfish can you see? Find them all and paint them yellow.

There are so many fish to see. How many can you count?

NOiSY DIFFERENCES

Spot six differences between these two pictures.

NOISY SHADOWS

Can you match the things with their shadows?
Draw a line with a crayon from the picture to its shadow.

NOISY MAZE

Pick your path and see where it will take you...

ANSWERS FOR PAGES 45, 46, AND 47

NOISY DIFFERENCES

NOISY SHADOWS

NOISY MAZE

1. The football player's trousers are purple in 2.
2. The American flag the boy on the left is waving disappears in 2.
3. A squirrel appears in 2.
4. The hot dog on the poster turns into a hamburger in 2.
5. A man in a red jacket playing the tuba appears in 2.
6. The man dressed as a hot dog, selling hot dogs disappears in 2.

1. The cheerleader takes you to the football player.
2. The howler monkey takes you to the rainforest leaves.
3. The flying doctor's plane takes you to the koala bear.
4. The racing driver takes you to his car.

Published in March 2015 by Lonely Planet Publications Pty Ltd.
ABN 36 005 607 983
www.lonelyplanetkids.com
ISBN 978 1 74360 780 0
© Lonely Planet 2015
Printed in China

Publishing Director	Piers Pickard
Publisher	Mina Patria
Art Director & Designer	Beverley Speight
In-house Senior Designer	Claire Clewley
Illustrator	Pippa Curnick
Author	Mark Conroy
Pre-press production	Tag Response
Print production	Larissa Frost

Thanks to	Lisa Eyre, Jessica Cole

Lonely Planet offices

AUSTRALIA
90 Maribyrnong St, Footscray, Victoria, 3011, Australia
Phone 03 8379 8000 **Email talk2us@lonelyplanet.com.au**

USA
150 Linden St, Oakland, CA 94607
Phone 510 250 6400 **Email info@lonelyplanet.com**

UNITED KINGDOM
Media Centre, 201 Wood Lane, London W12 7TQ
Phone 020 8433 1333 **Email go@lonelyplanet.co.uk**